SPIRITUAL INTERVIEW
WITH
LIU
XIAOBO

THE FIGHT FOR FREEDOM CONTINUES

RYUHO OKAWA

HS PRESS

Contents

Spiritual Interview with Liu Xiaobo
The Fight for Freedom Continues

Preface

Imprisoning a compatriot who has won the Nobel Peace Prize on charges of inciting subversion of state power, rather than treating him as the nation's pride, and censoring the news, so that the public would never know about it—these are the consistent character of the current Chinese government.

When people say on the internet that Chinese President Xi Jinping resembles Winnie the Pooh, the words "Winnie the Pooh" disappear completely from the information network in China. This is possible because their intelligence police alone has as many as 300,000 members and they constantly keep an eye on the internet. In a communist totalitarian nation that purges political adversaries, the devil's teaching of "dead men tell no tales" ought to be the first article of their constitution.

I do not think God will allow such an authoritarian nation to prosper. I want to protect the future of the people in Asia, Oceania, Africa, and Europe as well. As for Japanese people, they will not be able to protect their motherland without equipping faith as their shield. Now is the time.

Ryuho Okawa
Founder and CEO of Happy Science Group
July 23, 2017

Spiritual Interview with Liu Xiaobo

The Fight for Freedom Continues

Recorded July 21, 2017
Special Lecture Hall, Happy Science
Japan

Liu Xiaobo (1955 - 2017)

Chinese human rights activist and writer. Born in Jilin Province, China. He acquired an MA and a PhD in Chinese Literature from Beijing Normal University. The democratization movement began in Beijing while he was in the U.S. as a visiting scholar at Columbia University in 1989. He returned and joined the movement. In June of that year, he organized and conducted a hunger strike during the Tiananmen Square incident and was imprisoned on charges of counterrevolutionary propaganda and incitement. In 2008, he drafted and announced "Charter 08," which criticized the one-party rule of the Communist Party of China. Due to this, he was sentenced to 11 years imprisonment on the charge of inciting subversion of state power, back in 2010. In that same year, he received a Nobel Peace Prize while in prison.

Interviewers from Happy Science[*]:

Taishu Sakai
Special Assistant to the Chairperson
Religious Affairs Headquarters

Naoki Okawa
Advanced Executive Director
Second Secretarial Division
Religious Affairs Headquarters

Masayuki Isono
Executive Director
Chief of Overseas Missionary Work Promotion Office
Deputy Chief Secretary, First Secretarial Division
Religious Affairs Headquarters

[*] Interviewers are listed in the order that they appear in the transcript. Their
professional titles represent their positions at the time of the interview.

1

The Revolution for Freedom that Started at the Tiananmen Square

Many things were suppressed under the Cultural Revolution in China

RYUHO OKAWA

Today [July 21, 2017], I would like to attempt to record an openly recorded spiritual message from Mr. Liu Xiaobo, who passed away recently on July 13. He was a Chinese pro-democracy activist as well as a Nobel Peace Prize laureate. Articles about him were sometimes printed in recent newspapers, and they have been on my mind. But since there is not much information, I do not know much about him.

He and I are of the same generation. He is one year older than me. After graduating from undergrad and graduate school in China, he apparently went to study abroad in places like the U.S. In 1989, he came back after studying in the U.S. and joined the pro-democracy movement before the Tiananmen Square incident.

From May that year, he went out to Tiananmen Square, participated in the movement as a central figure representing intellectuals, and joined the hunger strike in the square. But on June 4, he was arrested during the

Tiananmen Square incident and prosecuted on charges of counterrevolutionary propaganda and incitement. He was then put in prison and removed from the public office register.

The year 1989 was about three years after Happy Science began its activities, so we were actually active at the same time. Some of you were probably not yet born at that time, or were still little.

The Tiananmen Square incident is a case that remains unclear. Before the incident, there was the Cultural Revolution [1966 - 1976], which ended in failure.

In 1949, Mao Zedong succeeded in his revolution and established the People's Republic of China. After that, he conducted military-first politics and prioritized military development. He also gave agricultural instructions to farmers. However, he failed in boosting Chinese economy, giving rise to a constant flow of people who could not support themselves. So, he was removed from power for a certain period of time. Then, with the Cultural Revolution, he succeeded in a counterattack and returned to power.

Later, the Gang of Four centered around Jiang Qing, who was one of Mao Zedong's wives and a former actress, continued the Cultural Revolution based on Mao Zedong ideology. In Japanese terms, it was similar to the Bunsei Reformation [1827 - 1829] that occurred in the Edo period; during that time, everything that was considered to corrupt the people, including kabuki, was purged. Likewise, during the Cultural Revolution, various cultures such as classical Chinese opera were suppressed, and many who were involved in culture and intellectual pursuits were also oppressed.

I have once heard a story directly from a Chinese woman who had her parents and relatives killed during the Cultural Revolution. She had fled to Japan and was living as a Chinese acupuncturist. According to her, it was a horribly cruel era; relatives were arrested, imprisoned and killed, one after another. Everyone had at least some family member or friend captured and killed. This very Gang of Four, however, was eventually banished and purged, too.

The Tiananmen Square incident revealed China's unchanged, old-fashioned regime

RYUHO OKAWA

Then, Deng Xiaoping came into power. Deng Xiaoping was a physically small man. I believe he went to study abroad in France. He had a sense for economy and adopted capitalism in the Chinese economy while maintaining communism in politics. To avoid committing the same kind of "mistake" that the USSR had made, he adopted the good sides of capitalism or liberalism only in the Chinese economy as he governed the nation under communism.

This kind of economic reform had already started in China when the Tiananmen Square incident occurred in 1989. Before this, a demonstration calling for democratization occurred in that large Tiananmen Square. Foreign media had come to cover it, and it was a sort of litmus test to see whether China would be able to democratize itself or not.

The year 1989 was exactly the same year that the Berlin Wall was torn down. I remember it well because I mentioned it in a lecture I gave that year[*].

At the time, Berlin was separated into West Berlin and East Berlin by the Berlin Wall. East Berlin was under USSR control while West Berlin was part of the liberalist world. Berlin citizens tore down this wall with picks and climbed over it. Police officers and other government officials were stationed at checkpoints, but massive waves of people climbed over the wall and the wall was smashed down. I saw that scene live on TV. I also went to see the actual spot two years later. So, 1989 was that kind of a year.

It was in that year that the pro-democracy movement started in China, and I wondered how it would turn out.

---

[*] The lecture, "Boundless Love" was given on November 12, 1989, published as *Boundless Love* (Tokyo: Happy Science, 2011), only available at Happy Science locations.

But with this incident, China revealed its unchanged, old-fashioned regime. They sent out tanks, running over and shooting the people involved in the democratization movement, killing people in droves. What is more, they cleared away all the bodies of the dead immediately, so we still do not know the number or the names of people who were actually killed in the Tiananmen Square incident. Due to this, the families of those involved could not even hold funerals.

This incident revealed that China is such a country. We knew that the Tiananmen Square incident occurred, but even the media from other countries were not able to report on the details. This really showed that the basic nature of China had not changed.

Liu Xiaobo, who was incarcerated for criticizing The government and received a Nobel Peace Prize while in prison

RYUHO OKAWA

Mr. Liu Xiaobo was a cultured person and one of the central figures of the pro-democracy movement. He was charged and incarcerated for counterrevolutionary propaganda and incitement in the Tiananmen Square incident. Liu was released in 1991. This was the year when Happy Science was officially registered as a religious corporation and when I gave my first Tokyo Dome lecture.

After he was released that year, he went underground while being called a traitor. He then secretly penned a memoir, *The Monologues of a Doomsday's Survivor* and released it. In May of 1995, he was detained again without being formally charged and was released in January of 1996. This was around the time Happy Science started constructing the head temples.

In the same year, he published an open letter criticizing the government and was sent to a forced labor camp in October, for re-education through labor. Then, in December 2008, he published "Charter 08" online, which called for a revision of the one-party rule of the Chinese Communist Party and demanded the freedom of speech and religion. Three hundred three Chinese scholars signed the charter. But just before it appeared on the internet, he was detained again.

In December 2009, he was charged for inciting subversion of state power and in 2010, he was sentenced to 11 years in prison and 2 years of deprivation of political rights. He was put in jail at this time. In December 2010, he received a Nobel Peace Prize praising his achievement of many years of non-violent fight for basic human rights in China [see Figure 1]. However, he was not allowed out of prison and had to accept the prize while in confinement. This was the first prize to go to a dissident against the Chinese government since the 14th Dalai Lama. The acceptance ceremony was conducted without him because he was in prison. He accepted the Nobel Peace Prize while staying in China.

In June 2017, Liu Xiaobo was allowed to leave prison on parole for treatment for terminal liver cancer, but passed away due to liver cancer on July 13. Before

Figure 1.
Liu Xiaobo's certificate and award left on an empty seat on the stage of the Nobel Peace Prize Ceremony. On the left is the Nobel committee Chairman, Thorbjorn Jagman (December 10, 2010).

he died, the West issued a request to take him out of China for treatment, but the Chinese government did not allow that. What is more, China cremated his body immediately after his death and scattered the ashes in the ocean because another counterrevolutionary movement could start if a large funeral were to be held. In other words, they did not allow a grand funeral ceremony or the making of a grave site because it would be trouble for the government if there was a place to worship him or if he was regarded as a hero. But their actions again attracted criticisms.

In Japan, a memorial service is held seven days after a person's death and apparently, China has the same tradition. The Chinese government did not want people to gather for his memorial service on the seventh day after his death, so they reportedly covered this up as well, trying to put a lid on it. This kind of information is slightly coming out of China now and again.

The books he wrote include titles such as *From the Tiananmen Square Incident to 'Charter 08': the Fight and Hope for Chinese Democratization* [in Japanese (Tokyo: Fujiwara Shoten, 2009)] and *The No Enemies Ideology: the Over 20 Year Fight for Chinese Democratization* [in Japanese (Tokyo: Fujiwara Shoten, 2011)].

So, this is the life of Liu Xiaobo, a person who was born in the same time as myself.

2

The Horror of China, A Country without Freedom

China claims itself to be a country under rule of law, But in reality a country under rule of man

RYUHO OKAWA

This morning, I did a little preliminary investigation because I wondered if a spiritual message from this person can only be carried out in Chinese or English. [Aide to Master] Shio tried hard to give an interview in Chinese and English, but it turned out that the spirit of Liu Xiaobo can understand Japanese. For us, that is convenient. It is important that Japanese readers understand his message. If it is translated into English, English-speaking people as well as some Chinese people will also understand. If it is translated into Chinese, then the message will get across to them even more.

To the Chinese government, this man was a bitter political enemy, an intimidating "malignant tumor" who actively attacked China's shameful aspects, or points of embarrassment. From the Western viewpoint, however, he was someone who deserved to receive a Nobel Peace Prize even while behind bars.

Recently, Xi Jinping went to Hong Kong and, in order to restrain Hong Kong's counterrevolutionary movement, stated that he would not accept anti-establishment forces, although he would allow "one country, two systems." This shows that China's stance remains the same. We want to know the facts on this point, but since we cannot get news from China, we do not know much about what is actually happening there.

When it comes to the news, reports from the West and Japan sometimes black out in China. Even the international broadcasting of NHK [Nippon Hoso Kyokai (Japan Broadcasting Corporation)] can be screened out immediately when the information is not favorable for the Chinese government. I have heard that the news of Liu Xiaobo receiving a Nobel Prize was also omitted. In fact, China has even gone so far as to create their own "Confucius Peace Prize" to compete with the Nobel Prize.

China has a law against counterrevolution, as well as a law against inciting subversion of state power. I'm sure Japan also has a law against overthrowing the government in its penal code [crimes related to insurrection in Article 77 of the Japan Penal Code]. For this reason, China may think of itself as a country based on rule of law, though I do not know if the Chinese people actually believe this or not. In fact, China distinguishes people as criminals, judges them and punishes them in some way, such as sending them to jail or to a forced labor camp, or executing them, all based on the laws they have made. However, we need to know that there is a little difference in the fundamental nature between what they think is "rule of law" and what Western democratic countries think is "rule of law."

Apparently, Xi Jinping is strongly enamored by Han Fei[*] and Shang Yang[†] of the Chinese Legalist School, which is one of the Hundred Schools of Thought. Many philosophers appeared in the era in which Confucius and his contemporaries were active, and they are called the Hundred Schools of Thought. The Legalist School included Han Fei, who wrote the book *Han Feizi*, and Shang Yang, who introduced changes to the law at the time. But Shang Yang was ultimately caught and killed based on the very criminal laws that he created.

This is actually a common occurrence. It is easy to make laws, catch people in that net, and rid people who are unfavorable to you. Thus, though China might call itself a country under rule of law, in reality, it is a

---

[*] Han Fei [ca. 280 - 233 BC] was a leading philosopher of the Chinese Legalist School during the Warring States period. As an envoy of Han, he was sent to Qin, but due to the slandering of Li Si, who once studied together with Han Fei and was the Chancellor of Qin, he was incarcerated and forced to commit suicide while in jail. His main work is *Han Feizi*.

[†] Shang Yang [390 - 338 BC] was a philosopher of the Chinese Legalist School during the Warring States period. He implemented various reforms in Qin dynasty, creating the foundation for the country's unification by the first Qin emperor.

country under rule of man. When the people in power make legal systems in a way that are favorable for them, they can arrest those who oppose them in one swoop or silence such adversaries.

A similar tendency can be spotted in Japan's current administration by the Liberal Democratic Party. When they passed the bill for anti-conspiracy law[*], I felt the same kind of danger.

The truth of communist nations: a storm of purges

RYUHO OKAWA

I can understand the idea of criminalizing anti-government forces, but China is a country that was established by means of revolution. It is kind of strange to criminalize anti-government forces when in fact the country was formed that way. If it were a crime, then there wouldn't have been the Chinese Communist Revolution in the first place.

Mao Zedong said, "Political power grows out of the barrel of a gun." This is one of his famous quotes, and it does not speak of peaceful means. According to Mao Zedong, a revolution does not come from words and debate, but out of the barrel of a gun; a revolution is

---

[*] Bill concerning the offence to criminalize an act in furtherance of planning to commit terrorism and other serious crimes.

preceded by an act of violence. In fact, he believed in the idea, "the end justifies the means." In that sense, his thoughts are similar to Machiavellianism.

This can also be found in Marxist thought. Marx said something like, "The use of violence is inevitable in the process to create a communist utopia, which is the ultimate goal. We can use violence as a means to achieve that goal." As a result, communist countries have experienced numerous cases of bloody purges from violent revolutions. That is a huge problem.

If you look at the French Revolution, which marks one of the beginning points of democracy, you can see that it was not only members of the royal ruling class who were met with death at the guillotine, but also the revolutionaries themselves. This involves an extremely difficult thought. I can understand the want to kill people who stand against you, but there is a huge problem with this way of thinking when we think about democracy.

The idea to purge people who stand in your way is very dangerous. In countries based on such a thought, there is always a struggle for power and most likely a storm of purges, although on the surface they may appear to be a democracy, gathering a large amount of people in a massive hall to discuss issues and electing a national chairperson by vote. This is why countries without the freedom of speech, the freedom of expression, the freedom of press, the freedom of religion, and the freedom of thought and belief, are frightening. Please know this.

Right now, a war of words and ideas is occurring Between countries without freedom And the Western world

RYUHO OKAWA

This problem of China's came about around the same time as when Happy Science started its activities. If China had not gone as far as to send out platoons of tanks to kill the citizens at the 1989 Tiananmen Square incident, it might have been possible for China to join the Western world. Nevertheless, if they had not skillfully carried out purges and suppressed speech at that time, they might have suffered the same fate as the USSR and collapsed, so it was indeed a major crossroads for China.

Anyhow, it appears that the Chinese economy is developing at an extremely high rate, but information is still controlled in China. For example, when the Liu Xiaobo incident was broadcast, the caricature of Xi Jinping in the image of Winnie the Pooh, a popular cartoon in America, was also on the internet. But all related information were immediately removed. I was surprised at how extreme the country was. During the Park Geun-hye administration in South Korea, a Japanese bureau chief for the Sankei Shimbun Newspaper in Seoul was indicted for defaming the president.[*] I was surprised by that incident, but China is no better than that.

So, there are countries that remove everything from information online to foreign TV broadcasts. As I have mentioned before, when I went on a missionary tour to give a lecture in Hong Kong in 2011[†], the hotel I stayed in was showing the Happy Science animated movie, *The Laws of Eternity* [Executive Producer Ryuho Okawa, released in 2006]. But when the movie got to the scene depicting the Spirit World, the screen blacked out and didn't show anything. I was astonished how far they could go.

A Happy Science animation broadcast on TV in Hong Kong was blacked out. They did not allow it to be broadcast because according to the Marxism-Leninism

---

[*] On October 2014, the Seoul Central District Prosecutors' Office indicted the former Seoul bureau chief for Sankei Shimbun Newspaper without arrest on charges of crimina lly defaming President Park under Article 70, Section 2 of South Korea's Act on Promotion of Information and Communications Network Utilization and Information Protection, etc.

[†] The author gave the lecture, "The Fact and the Truth" in Hong Kong on May 22, 2011.

materialistic view or the idea that considers religion as opium, the concept of the Spirit World is wrong. Even if these scenes are blacked out, people cannot complain or protest. We need to know that such is their actual state.

Despite that, China is now growing large. Many Chinese tourists come to Japan on shopping sprees, creating a trend in tourism. Japanese department stores have announcements in Chinese and salespeople that speak Chinese, and districts like Ginza and Shinjuku depend on Chinese spending. This may lead people to misconceive that China has now joined liberalist countries, but it is still doubtful whether they have changed in essence. In fact, the recent North Korean issue might have to do with this nature of China's.

A war of words and ideas is going on right now. As a result of this battle, will the Japan-U.S. alliance be pushed away by a new power and shrink to become one of the smaller powers of the world, or will the China-North Korea side go forward with their reform to Westernize, opening ways to talks on common ground? Or, will the current situation continue, each country only pursuing economic profit while insisting different political opinions? The answers to these questions will determine the future.

Summoning the spirit
Of a leading figure of revolution, Liu Xiaobo,
To hear his message of resurrection

RYUHO OKAWA

I have no idea what the spirit of Liu Xiaobo will say nor about internal information on China. We would like to ask him about that. We may later know how he is able to give a spiritual message in Japanese. But generally, many angels of light that have returned to Heaven can speak other languages, including Japanese. It is also true, from my past experiences, that strangely enough, devils that are active on the global scale can also speak Japanese. I don't know the reason for this, but they may have strong willpower. Ordinary spirits in Heaven or Hell cannot usually speak languages other than their own. But those with a strong wish to spread what they believe, be they in Heaven or in Hell, may be able to communicate their thoughts using willpower.

Liu Xiaobo may be seen as a devil to the Chinese government, but in the West, he was considered a leader of revolution. Today [the day this spiritual interview was recorded] marks the eighth day since his death, just past the "seventh-day memorial service" day in Buddhism. Of course, the resurrection of a person is something that should never happen in a materialistic country. But that is exactly why I believe his resurrection is meaningful.

We would like him to speak up if there is anything he would like to say about the Chinese government or if there is a message to the Chinese people. I believe that is what he actually wanted to say when he was alive. These would be the words of someone who could not get his message across through the media, and who could not leave the country. These would lead us to the questions, "How should we view the democratization movement?" and "What is justice in the international issues to come?"

China has now grown large. They have been expanding their military, trying to get their hands on Asian countries to the Arabian Peninsula, and as far as to Europe. They are rejecting American hegemony and trying to make Chinese hegemony. Is this simply a change in national power, the relative power between them? Or, does it mean there are problems from the viewpoint of global justice? We would like to find out more on this point. I hope we can get some good information today. So, let's try.

[*Closes eyes and puts hands together in prayer.*]

The spirit of the Nobel Peace Prize laureate,
Mr. Liu Xiaobo,
Who has recently passed away in China.
Could you come down to Happy Science

And reveal your thoughts to us?
Nobel Peace Prize laureate, Liu Xiaobo.
Please come down to Happy Science
And reveal your thoughts.
Please tell us your opinions, if any,
On China or the Chinese people,
Or even other countries including Japan.
We thank you in advance.

[*Approximately 15 seconds of silence.*]

3

The Resurrection of Liu Xiaobo:
A Passion for Freedom

"One-fifth of the world's population is in China, But human rights are virtually non-existent there"

LIU XIAOBO
[*Sways from side to side, resting his chin on his right hand.*]
Hmm, hmm.

TAISHU SAKAI
Are you Mr. Liu Xiaobo?

LIU XIAOBO
Eh? Hmm.

SAKAI
Are you Mr. Liu Xiaobo?

LIU XIAOBO
Yeah.

SAKAI
Thank you for coming here today.

LIU XIAOBO
OK.

SAKAI
I heard you could understand Japanese[*].

LIU XIAOBO
Yeah, I do.

SAKAI
OK. As Master Ryuho Okawa just mentioned, the Tiananmen Square incident occurred in 1989, the same year that saw the fall of the Berlin Wall. In my opinion, whether or not China would transform into a democratic country at that time was a major turning point in history. And I believe that you, Mr. Liu Xiaobo, were a key player in that turning point. In that sense, I think you are probably one of the people who hold the key to break the deadlock in the current chaotic world situation.

LIU XIAOBO
Hmm, OK.

---

[*] This spiritual interview was originally given and published in Japanese.

SAKAI

You have passed away recently, and we are now at a point in time [July 2017] just before the National Congress of the Communist Party of China, which is to be held this autumn, that would allow the Xi Jinping administration to start its second term.

LIU XIAOBO

Hmm, yeah.

SAKAI

You have left this world at such time. Is there anything you would like to say now frankly?

LIU XIAOBO

Hmm. China has a population of more than 1.3 billion people, which means it is home to one-fifth of the world's population. But it is oppressing its people to such an extent, and human rights are virtually non-existent there. In particular, there is no political freedom, no freedom of speech, no freedom of thought and no freedom of religion. Well, they do say they have freedom, but in reality, it is superficial. It is a formality. They say they allow various political parties to exist, and there are indeed small political parties, but it is just a formality to delude people. China is completely one-party rule and sticks to it. That is why there are fierce power struggles and purges still going on.

So, I think if God exists, He would not allow such a situation to continue in a country that has over twenty times the territory and ten times the population of Japan. Take, for example, the Berlin Wall that you just mentioned. Why were East Berlin and West Berlin so different? Post-war people learned from that gap. They were completely different, you know? And no one became unhappy by the collapse of that wall.

What's more, though young people may not know this, the many communist countries that existed in Eastern Europe, in the form of satellite states of the Soviet Union, were all liberated at the same time as the fall of the Berlin Wall.

The crucial point is that the people themselves are The objective of democracy

LIU XIAOBO

Of course, it may well be heartbreaking for those in power to see their country collapsing. However, comparing whether the single power-holder can act at will and whether its people can enjoy freedom and happiness is out of the question. I believe there are mistakes in the idea of Chinese revolution.

Its objective is to create a communist system itself, and gives no thought about whether that would result in the people's happiness. Moreover, the idea allows any means to achieve ultimate happiness which can give rise to unlimited oppression and purges.

So, here lies the crucial point, the critical point for someone who has studied in America: "People themselves are the objective of democracy. The very objective of democracy is to create a world in which people can work to achieve their goals, freely express their political opinions, engage in economic activities, and try tackling on all sorts of challenges without being discriminated against." I think Lincoln was of the same opinion. Its ultimate goal is to build a free society, so I believe there has been a mistake from the very start, in Marx's revolutionary ideology that shackles liberties and allows oppression to create a free society. I want to rectify this at all costs.

A lot of Chinese people go and study in America, but most of them are only studying about business and how to make money. When it comes to politics, they cannot do anything; they believe it is better to bend than break in the face of all-powerful one-party system. If they actually did take action, they would all end up like me. So, they are heavily brainwashed. Well, I suppose it is similar to what happens when religions launch "witch hunts."

The significance of Liu Xiaobo Launching a counter-offensive From Japan through a spiritual message

LIU XIAOBO

But someone must do it. I wanted to, but I couldn't because I was in jail. It was like the Ansei Purge[*] that happened in Japan in the mid-19th century; if all the revolutionaries were arrested and put in jail, they couldn't do anything. So, before anything, the authority would take away their freedom of speech and action. I wanted to lead a long life and work hard to spread the ideas that would change China into a free and democratic country, together with the efforts of Mr. Ryuho Okawa of Happy Science. It's such a shame...

SAKAI

So, was that your original aim in being born in the same time period as him?

---

[*] An oppression that occurred from 1858 to 1859 led by Naosuke Ii, against people who supported the *sonno joi* idea "respect the emperor and expel the foreign people." Well-known figures such as Sanai Hashimoto and Shoin Yoshida were imprisoned and/or executed.

LIU XIAOBO

Well, considering the number of people in China, I guess we were supposed to be killed, no matter how many revolutionaries were sent to earth. Many of our comrades have died in obscurity in prison execution grounds, and even now, there are many who are oppressed or chained in jail.

Still, I want to thank you for this occasion today. I don't know how widely this spiritual message will be conveyed in China, but this is equivalent to the resurrection of Christ. The Chinese government refused to hold a funeral or a seventh-day memorial service for me, and instead scattered my ashes in order to wipe me out completely, not leaving even my bones. Even so, I, Liu Xiaobo, am sending a spiritual message after my death.

China is a country that officially regards religion as opium even now. So, the fact that I am launching a counter-offensive from Japan is surely the equivalent, in both the religious and political sense, of some kind of revolutionary act. I want to offer some kind of encouragement, however little, to the comrades I have left behind, and to help those who will come after me, as much as I can.

4

Asking about the Truth of His Death In a Country without Human Rights

"We cannot stop a regime in which political Authority is completely combined with violence"

SAKAI

I suspect that quite a large number of people lost their lives during the Tiananmen Square incident.

LIU XIAOBO

Yeah.

SAKAI

So presumably, a lot of people actually had their close friends or relatives killed, but they, too, are keeping quiet about it, just as those who were involved in the movement for democracy are. Why is that? Why do they keep quiet after all that has been done to them?

LIU XIAOBO

Hmm... Well, of course, you cannot win against the armed forces, whatever people may say. In a government regime in which political authority is combined with military force, the freedom of speech and the freedom of thought and religion are not guaranteed. The freedom of expression is not guaranteed, either; once you oppose, they will come to arrest you in a heartbeat. Although you may say, "the pen is mightier than the sword," it will do you no good. Even if you go to America to write such things, you will be called a traitor and will not be trusted in China.

In a country like Japan, I suppose the state cannot implement such system of violence on people who speak out. Perhaps it does put some pressure on people who criticize the government, such as by inducing them to change their ideas or restraining them by using the police, prosecutors, or maybe the tax office. Yet, people can openly criticize the prime minister in magazines and newspapers, and on TV.

The authorities in China do not understand why it is good to allow such public criticism because for those people, being able to put their thoughts in action is the right thing to do. When building a bridge, for example, it won't get built if people keep arguing about it in the process. When the authorities decide to build a bridge, it is built. If they say they will build a dam, they will; they actually built the Three Gorges Dam*.

---

* A hydroelectric dam that spans across the Yangtze River in Hubei province, China. It is the largest power station in the world, with a capacity of 22,500 Megawatts. China regarded the dam as a great success and being eco-friendly, however, a flood displaced 1.3 million people and increased the risk of landslides.

If they use democratic means and allow for discussions, there would of course be a lot of opposition. That is why they believe, "We must take a strong attitude, otherwise our progress will be slow and we won't be able to achieve our targets. The state targets should come first. There would be no people without the state." Basically, this is their attitude. For the Chinese authorities, the state is most important and the people come second.

While you, Japanese people, may have various opinions on World War II, we should not regard everything about it in a positive light. Actually, in Japan, too, from pre-WWII to the end of it, there was the Special Higher Police that rounded up people involved in opposition movements one after another or arrested people for the books they possessed. If such a time had lasted for a long period, that would have been dark times indeed. And if the authorities killed the opposition before people knew anything about it, nothing would be able to stop such a regime. In such a situation, political authority is completely combined with violence. The average citizen is only armed with things like kitchen knives, spades and hoes. They might be able to get swords, but they can't beat the army with such weapons.

China had no qualms in sending tanks into the vast Tiananmen Square to crush protesters to death, even in the presence of the overseas mass media. This was really a shock to us, too. If they find people who try to disclose the truth, they will quickly jail and silence those people. So, everyone keeps quiet out of fear. The only other option is to make a successful escape to another country.

Chinese President Xi Jinping is acting quite Shrewdly to stay in power

SAKAI

Your death was very sudden. You died soon after the announcement that you were suffering from late-stage liver cancer, without being allowed to go abroad for treatment. This year, 2017, is a year when National Congress of the Communist Party of China will be held[*] and in fact, there are large-scale purges whenever it is held. Actually, Sun Zhengcai, who had been considered a candidate to succeed Xi Jinping as head of state, was purged in Chongqing.

LIU XIAOBO

Yeah, yeah. That's right.

---

[*] National Congress of the Communist Party of China is held once every five years. They discuss the country's major issues and pass resolutions, review the Party's Constitution, and select the Central Committee. The 19th National Congress is scheduled to be held in Beijing in autumn of 2017.

SAKAI

Should we consider you, Liu Xiaobo, to have died of natural causes?

LIU XIAOBO

Well actually, I was arrested and treated in a hospital that was under government patronage, so I did not know whether I was being given medicine or poison. After all, if I died from illness, that would be the end of the issue. If I had actually been executed, it would have caused uproar overseas, so death in hospital was convenient for them. They would be able to avoid being criticized by other countries.

As you pointed out, this year is when Xi Jinping would be assessed for the work he has done so far, so he had to oppress not just me, but my fellow democratic activists as well. He also has to settle economic issues. In fact, there are no real statistics in China, only "home-made statistics" or "fabricated statistics." Anyway, it is known that economy in China might be bubble economy with fictitious development. But if that were disclosed, it would be hard for him to stay in power, so he has been doing a lot to keep it concealed.

In addition to that, he has to clamp down on what seems to be an anti-government movement in Hong

Kong [see Figure 2], as well as divert people's attention away from the growing trend toward independence in Taiwan. It will be difficult for him to sever ties with North Korea and "hand them over" to the West while preventing Taiwanese independence. So, Xi Jinping is now acting quite shrewdly. He is incredibly wily. There are layers upon layers of intrigue.

Figure 2.
A march was held in Hong Kong to mourn the death of Liu Xiaobo (July 15, 2017).

5

The Historical Background that Created an Unusual Form of State

Sinocentric thinking, which holds that The world is tried under Chinese law

SAKAI

A few days ago, we received a message from the spirit of the Japanese sociologist Ikutaro Shimizu [1907 – 1988]. He said, "Actual conditions in China need to be clearly exposed. You need to keep sending cameras there and get people to state their opinions freely. That is what needs to be done*." Accordingly, we would like to hear from you today, Mr. Liu Xiaobo, about what you think needs to be revealed now. Please tell us your views on this point.

LIU XIAOBO

Hmm. Well, for more than a century, the Chinese people suffered various foreign invasions and were partially cut up and colonized. That history of over a century

---

* Refer to *Sengo Hoshu Genron-kai no Leader Shimizu Ikutaro no Shin-reigen* (literally, A New Spiritual Message from Ikutaro Shimizu, the Post-War Conservative Opinion Leader) (Tokyo: IRH Press, 2017).

led to their xenophobia and independence movement. This cannot be denied. It is true that they have a strong feeling of mistrust toward foreign countries.

Simply put, there is no such thing as international law in China. To them, national law is international law. Their idea has unified with the Sinocentric thinking of the past. They believe that China is the center of the world. It means that the world should be Sinicized and that the world is tried under Chinese law. In that sense, there may be some similarities with Islamic law. I suppose Muslims do not care about the Western legal system. Well, it is true to say that such a magnetic field exists in the world today.

To China, Japan has been a threat, As well as a mirror that reflects themselves

LIU XIAOBO

Japan is a tiny country, but it is a powerful state. Its presence has been a threat to China and, at the same time, a mirror that reflects us. We had to somehow catch up with Japan and overtake it.

The Opium War took place from 1840 to 1842, and after the war, various parts of China were cut up by the Western powers, who claimed that they were leased territories. But Japan went as far as to be on the brink of occupying the whole country. Japan was a terribly powerful country that had vanquished even Russia. There was the First Sino-Japanese War, but Japan was too strong. So, the Qing Dynasty was destroyed because they lost a war. After that, there were various twists and turns.

So, we lost the First Sino-Japanese War. If we combine the Second Sino-Japanese War and the Pacific War as part of the Pacific Theater of WWII in which America was involved, China could be considered one of the victorious nations, but that is not in fact true. China lost to the Japanese army at the time. The Kuomintang troops led by Chiang Kai-shek fled as far as Taiwan. Essentially, "China" was reduced to Taiwan only. The rest was no longer China.

Meanwhile, Mao Zedong and his followers [the Communist Party of China] emulated Liu Bei Xuande of *Records of the Three Kingdoms* and fled deeper inland, fleeing to western China. They fled as far as a mountainous region where the Japanese army could not come to attack them, as it would stretch the Japanese ranks too far. Up in the mountains, Mao and his followers kept moving their quarters from cave to cave. They kept a part of their forces hidden.

But when Japan was defeated, they swiftly came out and defeated Chiang Kai-shek's army, and the entire

China became communist. Although the Republic of China, or Taiwan, was initially a permanent member of the UN Security Council, the Communist Party of China [the People's Republic of China] took Taiwan's place because it was a big country.*

China displayed its ground war capabilities in The Korean War and the Vietnam War

LIU XIAOBO

At the same time, a mood of anti-communism arose and swept the United States known as McCarthyism.† People distrusted communism, and the plans for world order that were made at the end of WWII were practically scrapped just a few years after their conception.

In the Korean War, the ground forces of the Chinese army and the combined ground forces of America and South Korea clashed, and it was found that China was rather strong. The Vietnam War would probably not have

---

* In 1945, the United States, the United Kingdom, the Soviet Union, the Republic of China [ROC, now Taiwan] and other countries formed the United Nations, but the Republic of China was defeated by the Communist Party of China in the subsequent Chinese Civil War. While ROC retreated to Taiwan and maintained their government, Mao Zedong declared the formation of the People's Republic of China [PRC, also known as China] in 1949. Then, PRC replaced ROC as a permanent member of the UN Security Council.

† McCarthyism is an anti-communist movement that occurred in the 1950s, mainly led by the U.S. Senator Joseph McCarthy. The Second Red Scare. Politicians and intellectuals who were suspected of being communists were targeted.

happened without the 38th parallel armistice. Although some people may not know this, the Vietnam War broke out during President Johnson's term, and there was the "domino theory" at the time. Briefly put, it held that if the Communist Party of North Vietnam were to be left as it were, communism would spread to South Vietnam and then to other countries in succession. It was similar to the idea of cancer cells. To prevent that from happening, America decided to support South Vietnam in order to halt the spread of communism. But Ho Chi Minh and his followers [North Vietnam] were victorious because China moved south and provided them with military supplies, combat troops, and weapons. So, although China gained independence with the help of America in WWII, it fought America a few years later.

Even General MacArthur, who was in command during the Korean War, thought that China was an ally. He thought, "We helped them in WWII and they are our friends, so there is no way China will really commit to fighting us." He knew that there were Chinese troops on the North Korean side, but he thought that they were only few in number and that the enemy was mainly the Soviet Union. In fact, the Chinese army had advanced southward, and both North and South Koreas lost a million... well, the South probably a little less than a million. That is roughly how many casualties there were. I think there were probably between 1.5 million and 2 million deaths in the Chinese and North Korean armies. So, it became a major conflict, one on a par with the fight against Japan in WWII. This gave China confidence. They may not be able to win in aerial battles using "flying objects" or marine battles using ships, but they are confident that they wouldn't lose to the United States in a ground war.

The North Korean problem now won't turn out so bad as long as it is kept to a war of flying objects, or missiles, but there is no telling how many Americans would die if it develops into a ground war. That is probably why America is sounding out China so carefully. Well, that is how it is.

6

The Amazing Truth of the State and Its Worldview from the Perspective of A Chinese National

Chinese people have the attitude to take as much As they can get and not give anything

LIU XIAOBO

Oh no, I've lost the thread of what I was saying. What were we talking about?

SAKAI

I sought your idea on the key points we need to focus on in order to reveal the truth of China and democratize it.

LIU XIAOBO

Ah. Yeah. To democratize China... Hmm... Well you see, they aren't really aware that they are threatening other countries by expanding their military. The truth is that they believe in national particularism, so they do not care what they do as long as it is of benefit to their own country. As far as the Chinese are concerned, there is no misfortune in building up an army, occupying foreign islands, building maritime bases undersea, or taking Japanese islands. Their attitude is to get as much as they can. You think about things like "self-reflection based on international law" and "aggression," but to be perfectly frank, the Chinese don't have such concepts. Their attitude is the opposite of your teachings. "Take as much as you can. Receive as much as you can. Don't give anything. They took a lot away from us in the past. We were invaded and dispossessed. Now, we will take as much as we can get."

You speak of democratization, but the people support this greed, so that counts as democratization. Does that mean unleashing the starving masses to attack other countries? Well, maybe Japan has also done that in the past. The point is, the word democracy is totally ambiguous.

There is a terrible disparity between the Communist Party members who simply fill their Own pockets and other Chinese citizens

NAOKI OKAWA*

Based on what you have said, would it be correct to say that the Chinese citizens think the same way?

---

* Hereafter Naoki.

LIU XIAOBO

They have been lured. You see, there are a lot of people who have become rich. When the others hear that, they are duped into thinking they might get rich as well. There are in fact people who come to buy luxury items in Japan to take back home. And it's not just Japan. Nowadays, Chinese are everywhere, whether you go to Australia, Singapore, America, Canada, or Europe. Nouveau riches. Overnight millionaires from China keep buying up whatever they can get their hands on.

However, overall, it is maybe only 20% who have become rich, or should I say, who have become affluent. A portion of the population has been successful, and that is deliberately being put on display. On the other hand, since they believe their government policy is flawless and 100% correct, they totally reject anything that goes against it. "Progress and success means the government's policy being carried out as planned. Success for the state means success for the people."

So, the one equals the other. Simply put, it is a nationalistic way of thinking which holds that there is no happiness for the people without the success, progress and stability of the state. It is the thinking of the previous generation. This is the China today. As a small share of the country's benefits, those who are loyal to the Communist Party, and Communist Party members who have filled their own pockets, can go on extravagant junkets overseas.

NAOKI

It seems to me that such a way of thinking does not respect the human rights and freedom which you advocated at the risk of your life. I would like to hear your thoughts on what China should essentially do next, or your vision of an ideal China.

LIU XIAOBO

Hmm. Well, it is difficult because China is such a big country. In rural areas, up in the mountains, some people still live as if they are living in caves, even now. Conditions are harsh in farming villages, and there are still cases where they traffic their children. Like India, there are cases of children's internal organs being sold in China. Well, Beijing probably has no grasp of how things are in the country as a whole. They hold the Olympics and international expos, doing their best to put on a show, so that places such as Beijing and Shanghai look "modernized" to people from overseas, but they cannot do that for the entire country.

Why China is afraid of a multi-party system

LIU XIAOBO

You may not realize this, but actually, it makes the Chinese very uneasy and scared when we look at countries like Japan that are manipulated by the mass media, and where governments change according to whether they win or lose in the election.

Administrations change in America, too. China would be very scared if they had a two-party system where power moved between the two parties because the victors would be likely to purge the losers. They would fear for their lives. That is why the Communist Party members keep themselves safe by staying in convoy in a single-party system. The way they see it, there are fewer deaths by keeping things within the Communist Party. They are not sure how far the other party will go in a two-party or multi-party system.

This way of thinking is not easy to overcome. For example, this is similar to suggesting in Hitler's day that it would be a good idea to put forward two or three rivals to compete with Hitler. There is no way that would have worked [*laughs*]. An assassination squad would have leapt into action as soon as the rival's name came up. By the time information came in that someone was setting himself up as a rival to Hitler and was intending to seize power, the special police would already have taken steps to kill that person. This kind of thing goes on in China, too.

7

What is the Next Wave of Revolution? What Will Xi Jinping Do Next?

"There may be a revolution if more than half of the Population becomes affluent"

SAKAI

That is how China is now. How do you, Mr. Liu Xiaobo, see the future of China unfolding?

LIU XIAOBO

In terms of social ecology, I think that there may be a revolution if more than half of the population becomes affluent upper-middle and upper class people.

SAKAI

A revolution?

LIU XIAOBO

Yeah. Considering the number of people involved, I get the feeling that there might be a revolution, but it has not yet reached that stage. Hmm. Of course, overall, there are a lot of farming communities and the people in those places are poor. They are in poverty, which means that they have few educational opportunities and cannot acquire the capital to launch businesses that would lead to economic growth. China is trying to achieve success in the economy while keeping on with the same old ways in politics. But I cannot discount the possibility that a revolution will occur once they achieve some level of economic success and surpass the tipping point.

Where will the protagonists in this Revolution come from?

SAKAI
Who will be the protagonists or the base of this revolution?

LIU XIAOBO
Hmm. Well, it is hard to say since it would immediately implicate them in the crime of subversion of the state.

SAKAI
Ah. That is true.

LIU XIAOBO
You see, they have to continue as an underground organization until they have sufficient power to avoid being killed when they eventually reveal themselves.

SAKAI

In that case, is it correct to assume that there are still people there who have a specific spiritual connection with you, Mr. Liu Xiaobo? People who have come down to earth from the Heavenly Realm to cooperate with you?

LIU XIAOBO

I believe there are. And quite a lot, too.

SAKAI

I see.

LIU XIAOBO

There is in fact a group of people who have studied in America and another who has studied in Europe, and there seems to be some brainwashing among those people. However, they undergo reverse brainwashing with Sinocentrism and, as long as they obey that, they are used as state elite. The true elite are career members of the Communist Party who move smoothly up the ranks.

The "secondary elite" is made up of people who are among the cleverest in the country and who have studied in America. They went to a top-notch university there, or maybe earned an MBA from a graduate school and came back to take up important positions in the

Communist Party. In short, they are the people who went to America but didn't sell their souls. It's the people who simply studied to acquire knowledge and skills without selling their souls, and who apply their learning to develop their country, with a particular focus on economic development. In a sense, the second-tier elite is made up of hypocrites. Look at the current premier [Li Keqiang]. I think he is that type of person. In the end, he is the type of person that still cannot be fully trusted.

Xi Jinping is aiming to become "an emperor"

LIU XIAOBO
Well, in a way, Xi Jinping "awakened" at some point. I didn't expect him to go so far, but it seems he was rapidly awakened during the course of his actions. His aim was to rule over a unified China, but was suddenly driven by the desire to extend his rule as far as the Asia-Pacific region, Africa, Southwest Asia and Europe. I wonder whether it is due to some kind of spiritual guidance.

SAKAI
The Xi Jinping administration is about to enter its second term in office and it looks as though he is aiming for a third term. Another 10 years...

LIU XIAOBO

The thing is, he's probably aiming to become "an emperor." He's been watching Putin of Russia. Xi Jinping has seen how Putin is trying to extend his presidency further and is trying to use the same tricks.

SAKAI

It had been thought that President Trump would be his greatest rival, but Mr. Trump is having difficulties at the moment. What kind of influence would you like to see America having on China?

LIU XIAOBO

America is trying to democratize us, but it has fallen into the trap of democracy itself. The democracy trap is when the mass media possess too much information and are able to attack the government's weak points. Trump is being attacked like that. He is being attacked about things like "Russiagate." He needs to be on his guard all the time.

If it were happening in China, such media people could be executed as a bunch of traitors, which allows for a very stable government. Chinese people probably feel sorry for him. You see, they cannot understand what is good about all that. The Japanese prime minister probably wants to be like Chinese politicians. He probably wants to do as he likes in a world without opposition. Pfft [*laughs*].

8

The Astonishing State of China's Economy and Religion

The meaning behind the claim, "China's economic growth is a lie"

SAKAI

Currently, China is behind North Korea, which is creating problems. How should we resolve this? How would you, Mr. Liu Xiaobo, who knows the inner situation of China, think Japan should try to respond to this?

LIU XIAOBO

Well, Japan has not grown economically since the 90s, right? China has seen multiple times growth, has become the second largest economy in the world, and will grow larger than the U.S. China says so. Many Japanese citizens are being fooled, as are many people in foreign countries, too. Currently, there are some people, albeit not many, who are finally saying, "Maybe it's a lie that China is the second largest economy and Japan is the third?" There are opinions that say, "Japan is still the second [largest economy], and China is the third. Maybe the statistics are lies?"

Well, if we were to come up with a national goal, in the end, each province will fabricate its own statistics to match the goal. If the central government can total all of these numbers, it can seem as though the economic progress meets the national goal. This is because there isn't a third party overseeing these activities.

In the past, there was a way to torture captives in prison without sentencing them to death. They would simply dig a hole all day. The following day, they would fill the hole, and the day after that, they would dig it again, only to be filled again the next day. Then, in a month, they would go crazy. Like this, China seems to be putting all their efforts into making up pointless economic statistics.

I do not have the resources to collect material, so I wouldn't know, but perhaps the economic progress in China is something that becomes as planned. If the Chinese government were to extend the deadline, just as the Japanese government did with their goal of two-percent economic growth because they couldn't accomplish it, the Chinese government would suddenly be met by a political crisis. This is why they always seem to achieve their goal.

So, you must ask yourself how much you can trust these numbers. If you are growing seven, eight percent a year, you will grow in multiples, economically, very quickly. In other words, like the prisoner example, they may be "completing the task, breaking it down. Completing the task, breaking it down. Completing the task and breaking it down." They may be just continuously repeating tasks and saying, "We built a factory, the economy has grown larger." "We tore it down, and there are economic effects to doing it." "We built it again. The economy has grown larger." "We tore it down again, and the economy has become smaller." "With this, there will be economic effect." Perhaps they are doing things like this repeatedly.

SAKAI

Conversely, this is where the weakness of China lies, right? From the anti-Chinese perspective.

LIU XIAOBO

In a nutshell, China is a dictatorship. In a dictatorship, opposition is not allowed. It does not allow a third-party organization or competitor. It does not allow critics and journalists any freedom. If they say anything unnecessary, they would be killed immediately.

In China, the reality is that those in power Do not keep each other in check

SAKAI
Recently, the spirit of Ikutaro Shimizu said, "You have to expose the Chinese paradox. You need to verify whether truly capitalistic developments are being made or not in a communist country."

LIU XIAOBO
I believe that the former Soviet Union was similar. It's easier to figure out the statistics for heavy industries that practice planned production. However, statistics in the field of commerce is very unclear. Various stores have various account books, and nobody knows if these account books are all true. If somebody comes to verify the books, but is bribed under the table and turns a blind eye, the story ends there. China has been like this from the long past. This is why their commercial information is unclear. Their trade relations are in the dark too, since bribery is widespread. So realistically, we don't know how much of it is true. We don't.

Politically, those who confirm these statistics or people who have licensing rights to trade, namely politicians including local ones, take bribes and fill their own pockets. It won't happen in Japan, but in China, mayors of regional municipalities can pocket about 4 billion yen. This would be quite difficult to do in Japan, since the tax office will probably come in. However, in China, the tax office, municipal office and the mayor are all part of the same power structure. They are connected. They are friends. With this, in reality, those in power do not keep each other in check.

Although, if there were orders from the top, it can be done. "Expose that person's wrongdoings," the top would say. Well, various information makes its way to the top. As long as they are swearing loyalty, the top won't do it. However, they have the information, so the question is when those subordinates' loyalty is under suspicion. Are they meeting up with rebellious factions or democratization activists like us? Or, if the fact that they offer financial funding is revealed, the security police will move in to quickly arrest and put those people in prison.

China's underground religions

SAKAI

In China, I believe a lot of country-changing revolutions occurred due to religion. Would you speak about the tasks that religion must accomplish right now?

LIU XIAOBO

Well, about this, hmm... Since the Opium Wars during the Qing Dynasty, Europeans sent Christian missionaries as the vanguard and then they later came to occupy that area. Once they were allowed missionary activities through the freedom of religion, they produced numerous believers, which then transformed into political power. Following this, the land would be taken by foreign countries and power would be stripped away from authority. There were many such cases. Empirically, religion has been used in this way, so China won't easily let their guard down.

This is why official or public religions are under national surveillance. Religions are all treated similar to how the Aum Shinrikyo [a cult in Japan], is treated in Japan. There are probably about five public religions, but they are all under national surveillance. There are a few underground churches, but even these are all researched by the security police. They are already prepared to round them up in case they look like they will revolt. Prime Minister Abe probably saw this and hurriedly set conspiracy as a crime.

Further, there was an era where unorthodox religions like the White Lotus became popular. This is why even the "foreigner-expelling" movement cannot be trusted fully, even though it's a patriotic religion. In the end, they will trick the citizens, make their way into state authority, and enjoy the benefits from that. The Chinese have experienced many of these kinds of evil religions.

In the end, even Christianity may help spread European imperialism. If a Japanese religion went right in, who knows when it might fall into the hands of Japanese imperialism. The Chinese constantly hold onto a sense of danger in this regard.

Only religion can go against immense state power

LIU XIAOBO

It's just that, I don't think there is anything that can go up against immense state power besides religion.

SAKAI

Only religion, you say?

LIU XIAOBO

Only religion can take the risk of speaking justice without fearing death. In history, there have been dangers when foreign religious organizations came in, but through these, there were exchanges of information between foreign and domestic believers. With this, the domestic believers will find out what their country is doing wrong or what they are hiding. Numerous books of Happy Science are now coming into China. There are a lot of books coming in and various information is flowing in. So, we have some hope.

SAKAI

What would, for example, be the role of religion in Japan to act as a barrier that will protect us from China's hegemony?

LIU XIAOBO

From China's point of view, there are no differences between Japanese religions and Japanese political system. It looks as if they are working alongside each other, so there isn't much distinction between the two.

9

His Conviction Goes Beyond Death

Where does Mr. Liu Xiaobo's aspirations and Driving force come from?

MASAYUKI ISONO

I would like to ask you a question from a different angle. We are now nearing the 30th anniversary of the 1989 Tiananmen Square incident. Earlier, you mentioned that if a nation with an army oppresses its people, the citizens are helpless and the only path would be for them to surrender or submit. Even so, Mr. Liu Xiaobo, you lived with the conviction to give people various freedom through democratization and to create a happy society in the past 30 years, although you, yourself, were deprived of freedom. Where did the driving force that supported your conviction come from?

LIU XIAOBO

Well, my study abroad in the U.S. played a big part of it. If you learn political ideologies too well, oftentimes it is quite dangerous. America is a free country to some extent. In terms of equality, it is a country that gives you the right to challenge yourself, whether you are a woman, a black person, or an immigrant. This ideology left a strong impression in me.

In terms of equality, I believe there is a slight difference in how we think. The current leader Xi Jinping, although he went to the U.S. for a little bit, he only went there for agricultural seminars or something like that, so I don't think he learned much about political ideologies. During the Cultural Revolution, he was sent to the countryside of China, as a part of the government policy to send city elites to the countryside to experience poverty in a farming region. In other words, I believe they were trying to make the citizens tougher by having them live in poverty and preventing them from complaining. He probably experienced this.

Well, he may understand a bit of various things, but once he assumed the position of authority, maintaining the authority became his goal and purpose. I think he is now very much enjoying his position. It must be so much fun for him to watch Europe and the U.S. fear China growing bigger, and to watch Japan frozen like a hare.

The truth behind the words, "I have no enemies"
In his speech at the
Nobel Peace Prize award ceremony

ISONO

I would like to ask you another question. When you received the Nobel Peace Prize in 2010, you were in prison and were unable to participate in the award ceremony. During the ceremony, your message was read and it mentioned, "I have no enemies."

LIU XIAOBO

Yeah.

ISONO

You mentioned the following. "But I still want to say to this regime, which is depriving me of my freedom, that I stand by the convictions I expressed in my June Second Hunger Strike Declaration 20 years ago—I have no enemies and no hatred. None of the police who monitored, arrested, and interrogated me, none of the prosecutors who indicted me, and none of the judges who judged me are my enemies."

LIU XIAOBO

Yeah.

ISONO

Against a person, nation or government who deprived you of your own freedom and made your life unhappy, you would usually be filled with hatred, anger or revenge. Yet you attained the level of forgiveness, which is a very religious state, by saying that you have no hatred and you have no enemies. Did you have any religious beliefs? If not quite religious, did you hold value in some spiritual ideas?

LIU XIAOBO

Well, you could say I was religious, but I was also pragmatic. Dr. Martin Luther King, Jr. of the U.S., with his movement to give rights and equal treatment to blacks, refrained from using violence. He was a pacifist, and he realized that violence would not pay. If he fought back with violence, the white people and the white police officers would come back with even more violence, which would endanger themselves.

Gandhi of India was the same. As somebody who had seen what was happening in England and South Africa, he believed that the problem could not be overcome using violence. He believed that if he used violence to defeat some English people, he would only face retaliation by military force and would suffer even more. We, the peaceful activists and pro-democracy activists in China, are the same. Even if we stand up to fight with machine guns, the government would purge us using much more intense military forces. It's obvious.

With those words, I meant to discipline myself, as well as admonish my fellow activists not to be so hasty. A violent revolution against a nation that was established as a body of violence would only result in the massacre of all involved. What is essential is how you nurture the existing little "buds of democracy." You must spend time making them grow, avoiding storms as much as possible.

Our comrades are those who went overseas and came back, and through information they acquired little by little, started to reform themselves. There are also people who have changed their ways of thinking after becoming affluent themselves, or through information by international media that comes in little by little. Having such people come forth helped a lot.

In a way, the situation is similar to Japan during the Meiji Restoration. Through exam studies and earning an academic background, or through studying abroad, people have a better chance of getting a good job. So, I thought that as long as we do not come under extreme oppression, we might be able to achieve a revolution gradually. You know, we have to look at a span of one generation or about 30 years in building up our forces. A rapid revolutionary movement would subject us to oppression and dissolution in a single blow. We would be wiped out without a trace.

China is a scary country. We have nuclear weapons, so even foreign countries cannot speak their opinions freely. There are people who want to rely on Japan's power, but there is a rush of anti-Japanese movies. Movies and TV dramas are mostly of such content. So, no one can openly ask for Japan's help.

If a single grain of wheat dies...

SAKAI

Just now, you mentioned about the Meiji Restoration. Why did you, Mr. Liu Xiaobo, choose to be reborn in China in this current era?

LIU XIAOBO

Well, I didn't think I could cause a revolution by myself. However, I did think that I could at least be a valuable sacrifice. Although this may sound Christian, I thought, "If a single grain of wheat dies..."* By abandoning my life and falling to the earth, there could be new fruit. This is the feeling I had.

Just a single grain of wheat is not enough to change a huge country like China. Hundreds of lives, precious

---

* Words of Jesus Christ in the New Testament. "Truly, truly, I say to you, unless a grain of wheat falls into the earth and dies, it remains alone; but if it dies, it bears much fruit." [John 12:24, English Standard Version])

lives, need to be given up, otherwise we cannot make it happen. We do not know the exact number of deaths in the Tiananmen incident. Some say four to five thousand, while others say about one hundred thousand, but nobody knows. Such kind of information completely disappears in China.

In the past, there was an incident where a high-speed train derailed in China [in 2011][see Figure 3]. When the train fell from the overpass, people were still inside. Although there were people still alive and hurt, a hole was dug in the ground and the entire high-speed train was buried out of fear of being covered by international media. This is their basic attitude.

Figure 3.
A derailed high-speed train being taken down after a collision which happened in Wenzhou, Zhejiang province, China, on July 24, 2011.

10

His Soul is an Eternal Revolutionist

Past life as a Japanese patriot who was executed The Night before the Meiji Restoration

SAKAI

We will turn to a spiritual topic. If you were born in Japan in your past life, may we assume that it was during the Meiji Restoration?

LIU XIAOBO

Well, it hasn't been long since I died, so my answer won't be so accurate. But yeah, that's how I feel.

SAKAI

Assuming you were alive during the Meiji Restoration, were you someone that was involved with the Ansei Purge, one of the incidents that triggered the Meiji Restoration?

LIU XIAOBO

...hmm. I have heard of notable names such as Mr. Shoin Yoshida. Yes, I have. I've also heard of Mr. Shonan Yokoi and Takamori Saigo. Mr. Katsura and Kusaka too. Yeah.

ISONO
Which feudal clan were you in at the time?

LIU XIAOBO
Hmm? Yeah [*approximately 5 seconds of silence*]... Well I died as a Chinese man, so even if you ask me, well...

SAKAI
Before recording this message, the name "Sanai Hashimoto" briefly came to Master Ryuho Okawa's mind.

LIU XIAOBO
Hmm... Yeah that name sounds familiar. Ah. It does. Yeah.

SAKAI
Aren't you Sanai Hashimoto himself?

LIU XIAOBO
Hmm. Hmm. I just died, so I'm not completely sure. But that name does sound, hmm, hmm, hmm, hmm, hmm...

NAOKI
He wrote *Keihatsu-roku** at the time...

---

* A book written by Sanai Hashimoto when he was 14 years old. It contains his aspiration in life.

LIU XIAOBO

In the past life, I spent some time in prison. But I think I did some activities in my youth. I remember saying something like, "Abandon your childish heart (in Keihatsu-roku)"...

SAKAI

Ah, so you are Mr. Sanai.

LIU XIAOBO

I wasn't able to accomplish anything important. I was only involved with the administration of the politics of the feudal clan for a period of time. That's about it.

SAKAI

But in truth, it is what started off the new era.

LIU XIAOBO

That's not the case. It was the work of about a few thousand patriots of the revolution.

SAKAI

However, the Ansei Purge was one of the biggest incidents. In this life as Liu Xiaobo too, you passed away in prison, so it's almost the same situation.

LIU XIAOBO

Well, I am the first Chinese (in China) to receive a Nobel Peace Prize during imprisonment. This means that foreign countries will remember me as a recipient in prison.

So, the Chinese government is currently afraid of the movements that say, "Don't let Liu Xiaobo's death go to waste." I bet they're most afraid that this movement will occur within China or that the movement will invite support from overseas.

If I had lived a long life and become the President of the Republic, it would have been bothersome for them. That would have made a Mandela. It would have been troublesome for them if I had become a Nelson Mandela. So, they had to kill me by all means. I'm not even sure if they actually treated me. Hmm.

A spiritual connection to Yukio Mishima?

SAKAI

I would like to know another thing. Do you have any spiritual connection to Yukio Mishima*?

---

* (1925-1970) A Japanese author and playwright. He carried out right wing political activities in his later years. Refer to *Tensai Sakka Mishima Yukio no Egaku Shigo no Sekai* (literally, The Life After Death Depicted by Yukio Mishima, A Gifted Author) (Tokyo: IRH Press, 2012).

LIU XIAOBO

Yukio Mishima... Hmm... [*approximately 5 seconds of silence.*] He was born a while before me, but we lived roughly in the same time... hmm. There must be a group of spirits that's interested in patriotism and national defense. I had some kind of connection with them, but I was born in China, so I couldn't have been born as Yukio Mishima in Japan at the same time.

I'm sure he caused a movement to promote Japan's independence, a country virtually colonized by America, brainwashed and unable to be independent as a nation, although Japan and China are reversed on how an independent nation should be. But I think there was some commonality in what we wanted to achieve. Our lives may have crossed paths in a previous life, but since I didn't even get a funeral, I can't go that far back. I don't know.

11

The Truth about the Human Rights Situation and the National Identity of China

China only has one percent as much Human rights as the U.S. does

SAKAI

There is a chance that from now on, you will become a symbol of revolution as a pioneer of the era. Therefore, I would like to ask you to give a message to the Chinese citizens that will follow you.

LIU XIAOBO

Well, the Chinese government is the same as how the Japanese army used to be. They continue to broadcast government propaganda and brainwash the people. They do not release information that is unfavorable to them. Quite frankly, China is the nation that gave birth to North Korea. North Korea is a rogue country that China bore. They think, "We're copying what China did, so what's the problem?"

Now, China wants to join the G7, so they are making efforts to make themselves seem they can adapt themselves like a chameleon, but there are some parts they cannot hide. Many foreigners came into China during the Olympics and the World Expo, so China tried hard to show their good side only. They made efforts to make sure that the cities, including the surrounding areas, where people would visit for the Olympics and the World Expo, looked good without revealing their true state. What is more, they did not allow the mass media do any coverage elsewhere without permission.

North Korea is probably similar. The coverage of just Pyongyang and its surrounding areas does not reveal the truth, but there are certainly many problems. If the mass media could record the voices or videos of people's complaints and dissatisfaction, many problems will surface. But a lot of people there don't even have any information to base their judgment on whether they're being mistreated in the first place.

Still, many Japanese factories have come into China. Not all Japanese ideologies make their way in, but it is true to say that the Japanese factories are an example as to how our goals should be in our management and economic progress. So, surprisingly, people know very well. They know surprisingly well about the driving force behind Japan's progress.

In Japan, only a few media reported that China bought and modified a second-hand aircraft carrier from Russia [Ukraine]. In contrast, when Japan deployed a helicopter carrier, "an aircraft carrier" which is called a destroyer in Japan, a destroyer like an aircraft carrier, the news spread all over China at once, and most Chinese people know about this. Ironically, few Japanese people know about it. Such things can happen, so it's difficult to keep the Chinese mass media, which are a mixed bag of truth and lies, under control.

But the major problems in China are that the law is not right, the justice system is not right, and human rights have very little value. Human rights have little value in China; it's as if a Chinese person's life were equivalent to only one-hundredth of an American person's life, so our lives are barely protected. Well, since we have a large population, they could say that the value of each person is dropping due to an inflated population. However, we need to make this a country where the value of each person is respected more.

The Chinese government is now seeking various resources in foreign countries and trying to share their benefits with people who can no longer bear the poverty. In this regard, rather than forever stressing on the damages they were inflicted in the past, they should know more about the current international opinions and what they are being criticized for.

The national character of China: The tendency to justify oneself

LIU XIAOBO

You know, the Chinese citizens do the complete opposite of what you, Happy Science, teach as a religion. They are very eager to defend themselves, while at the same time, very zealous about attacking others. So, when they hear the Happy Science teaching, "Give love to others and reflect on yourself," they feel they wouldn't even be able to protect themselves. When they are caught, they will definitely be regarded as criminals, so they have a habit of telling others how right they are. You could say this is the national character of China.

Chinese people might be disliked by people of other countries, but in China, people will see you as below average if you can't even defend yourself. Therefore, it's a matter of whether or not the world can accept this as China's national character.

China does not want to bring in Japanese culture

LIU XIAOBO

It is believed that sense of humor can nullify this tendency. In contrast, Japanese people seem to show less expression, so it is hard to understand how they feel.

Compared to the Japanese, the Chinese will give logical rebuttals.

Even so, they go on shopping sprees. Apparently, many Chinese people go to Japan, but they don't want to bring in Japanese culture. Just buying products is fine for them, I guess. In China, there are lots of imitations of brand name goods, so they buy genuine products in Japan and sell those to make money. These kinds of activities are rampant. Nevertheless, they are somewhat affected, so they understand the greatness of Japan. Yet, they really want to boast about their own country.

In the end, we need to measure Japan and China using the same set of standards. For example, utilizing the same standards to measure both economies, or revealing how much hidden military capabilities they both have.

China is now confident that they would win in ground battle, whether the enemy is the U.S. or Japan. However, they still think they would lose in marine or air battle, so they can't stop their militarization yet. As for the Chinese government, they don't want mainland China to be put in a crisis through the North Korean issue. This is a concern for them.

In China, matters like the Kake Academy problem are commonplace

LIU XIAOBO

One of the elements in my pro-democratic movement was the effort to give more respect to human life. This requires due process of law. For a trial, one must be guaranteed satisfactory legal procedures. Fundamentally, criminal law must be applied based on the presumption of innocence, thereby protecting human rights. Arbitrarily created laws must be checked by the international community, of course. If China does not understand this, they should allow the mass media to speak freely and give people materials on how they should view an issue.

In Japan, the weekly magazines and other media are criticizing the weaknesses in the government or the weaknesses in the opposition parties, trying to bring them down. In a way, this is pitiful, but in another way, it means that the authorities are constantly under watch for corruption. For some people, their human rights are being violated, but in a larger sense, I feel it is serving to protect the human rights of the common people.

Something like what is happening in Japan now about how the Abe administration provided advantages to their friends[*] is quite commonplace in China [*laughs*].

---

[*] This is referred to as the Kake Academy problem, now taken up by various mass media in Japan (at the time of recording).

If something like this becomes a problem, well... If someone made tens or hundreds of billions of yen, then it can become a problem, but the fact that only a million or two in donations or some political support were given to those who are at the nation's top-level positions will be covered up immediately. They won't get kicked out for something like that.

We are now made to believe that China is run under the rule of law, but we should try as much as we can to speak about the problems of Chinese law from different perspectives, and add in the issues revolving how to guarantee human rights. As for economic problems, we must weed out those who are lining their pockets through sly methods by strictly applying the principles of fairness and equality. Xi Jinping is also probably accumulating wealth and is stowing away his assets overseas through his relatives, but I hope these practices will all be cleansed.

The Chinese government is unable to make their citizens equally wealthy. As a communist nation, they should be doing this, but they cannot. That is why they are trying to exploit wealth from other countries or make a handful of people in the country to be their scapegoat and say, "These people were doing bad things." They would execute them as a warning to others, and try to silence complaints. They are currently using such an outdated method.

Will anyone be able to stop Xi Jinping, Who is thinking about controlling Europe, Africa And the oil fields region?

LIU XIAOBO

China is not a country that will change so easily. Xi Jinping is aiming to become an emperor, and in terms of planning ability, he surpasses the past presidents. He is probably thinking about surpassing Mao Zedong. He is thinking about trying to rule Europe and even turn Africa into a colony. Furthermore, he also wants to put the entire oil fields region under his control. The U.S. retreated significantly during the Obama administration, so I wonder if anyone can stop China. But even if someone could stop China, I'm not sure if things will improve after that.

A unified China has always been our earnest wish. However, there will always be victims that come with the goal of unification. Chinese history is full of internal warfare. So, there are actually many people who think it's better for Liu Xiaobo to be thrown in prison or die than to have internal warfare start up and draw out again.

12

A Message to the Chinese Revolutionaries

The Chinese government's biggest enemy is religion — Spread thoughts and ideas

LIU XIAOBO

You definitely need a thought, or an idea. I don't know if your thoughts can help this situation, but please give rational reasons as to why humans have dignity. Also, explain completely how to be wealthy.

Please teach that it is not necessary to follow the Western way in order to become wealthy, and that it is possible to achieve this the Eastern ways. If you do a good job in teaching those, your thoughts will enrich and make the Chinese people wealthy.

I bet that the government's "biggest enemy" is religion. In China, what's only a Qigong group are being oppressed since they announced that they have 90 million members. But such a group with no thoughts will not be able to overturn the government. So, I think what we need is some power that has a base outside China and envelop it with a global movement. Now, the most likely power would be the underground churches, which [in China] have been estimated to have over one hundred million members. I think that the possibility of a revolution by Christian is extremely high.

I think you guys have a chance as well. Your thoughts are now spreading through Taiwan, Hong Kong, and other areas. The Chinese are quite receptive about what's trending in Japan, so there are a large number of people who know of Ryuho Okawa.

Also, instead of revolutionaries that get slain in China one after another, find more international ones. Instead of "proletariats of all nations, unite," replace that with "Happy Science members from all nations, unite." I'm not exactly sure myself, but all I know is that you guys are producing something that will become a "mediator" or "cushion" or a bridge between the East and West or with Islam. But before that, I don't know how many of those participating in the democratization movement will become victims, but break down the dictatorial regime. Also, please teach the Chinese people what true power means.

Create infrastructures for your thoughts or activities To use as ingredients for the revolution

LIU XIAOBO
I am "Liu" and I hear the name "Liu Bei" throughout this organization. If you say that the heroes of *The Three*

Kingdoms have been born in Japan, you should use them as tools in your missionary work. If you spread that the heroes of The Three Kingdoms are born in Japan and are teaching such and such, it may actually trend.

To you, it may be no more than an old-fashioned play, but maybe you guys can create a modern version of The Three Kingdoms, export it, and change their mindset by showing that you're with the Chinese.

"A Spiritual Interview with Liu Xiaobo" might not have much worth. It might be better to record spiritual interviews with older, greater figures, translate them to Chinese, and publish them. From that, reveal that "According to those figures, something's not right about China."

China is a Buddhist country as well as Confucian. It has many philosophies, including Taoism. I heard that Chuang-tzu is a part of Happy Science. I heard that it includes the philosophies of Lao-tzu and Chuang-tzu, and the teachings of Confucius, too. So, if you come in by using the Chinese philosophy skillfully, you might be able to create another path[*]. I believe now is a difficult

---

[*] Refer to *Kokai Reigen Roshi no Fukkatsu Soshi no Honshin* (literally, Spiritual Interview: The Resurrection of Lao-tzu and Chuang-tzu's True Thoughts) (Tokyo: IRH Press, 2012) *Soshi no Jinsei-ron* (literally, Chuang-tzu's Theory on Life) (Tokyo: IRH Press, 2014) *Roshi no Kofuku-ron* (literally, Lao-tzu's Theory on Happiness) (Tokyo: IRH Press, 2014) *Koshi no Kofuku-ron* (literally, Confucius's Theory on Happiness) (Tokyo: IRH Press, 2014) *Koshi "Kairiki Ranshin" wo Kataru* (literally, Confucius Speaks on Supernatual Phenomena) (Tokyo: IRH Press, 2014) *Sekai no Choryu wa Konaru* (literally, The World Will Trend in this Way) (Tokyo: The Happiness Realization Party, 2010).

time, since you are taking a stand to politically oppose nuclear weapons and North Korea, which is leading the government to be cautious of you. But I think it's important to do a better job in creating a philosophical base or philosophical infrastructure that can help the public think of a new revolution.

They should be cornered from the south. Do what you can to keep a stronghold of Taiwan and Hong Kong, then spread out a bit more into Southern China, then into the city. I think this kind of strategy is important. It will be good for you guys to have some factories as allied enterprises. Disguise as a manufacturer and "export" the factory and transform it into a missionary work house. I think it's plausible.

You should just go ahead and do missionary work to UNIQLO. Convert them all into Happy Science. In that case, you will get many Chinese members. There are quite a few others. So, you guys should put in a little more effort in this area. I think so. What do you think?

A new revolution —
Spread the mind that loves diversity and tolerance

SAKAI
Thank you very much. We would like to take your words and spread them through all of China and Japan.

LIU XIAOBO

I think that now is the time for a new revolution. A revolution, or a counterrevolution, can be seen as a crime. But there are things that cannot be done with just one idea so you should teach that it is important to learn from others what should be learned, and that important ideas are currently being taught in Japan. There are teachings that are not opposing the West, so I think it is also important to learn these. The number one characteristic of Happy Science is tolerance. Diversity and tolerance. The teaching on diversity and tolerance will lead to democracy.

Just preaching on unity alone won't create a democracy. Being unified leads to totalitarianism. So, tolerance and a mind of love or a mind that loves diversity. A mind that loves diversity is a mind that allows the era of Hundred Schools of Thought. You should face them head on with a philosophy such as, "The true God wishes for many philosophies to bloom in profusion like the Hundred Schools of Thought which will bring the country to wealth." It would be troublesome if a rule like Qin Shi Huang of Qin dynasty continues for a long time.

The next decade will be crucial for the battle Between America-Japan and China-Korea

LIU XIAOBO

The next decade is crucial. It will be like a sumo wrestling match. The Japan-American alliance versus Chinese hegemonism and North Korea. These ten years will decide who will get thrown out of the wrestling ring. So, this is your era. How will you fight during the ten years of your era? The Liu Xiaobo wave is just a milestone. Next, you must increase the number of people who take action with the Happy Science teachings as their backbone.

First, it's important to take back freedom of speech and press, freedom of expression, etc. Of course, it is important to take back freedom of religion, philosophy and creed, and political creed at the same time. Even freedom of religion is written in China's constitution, but they do not follow it. It's not far off from saying, "Even the Aum Shinrikyo, has freedom of religion." Well I am curious about the religion of Happy Science as someone who lived in the same era. So, I pray that it will become a fuse for the new Chinese revolution of some sort. So, without hesitation, please bring back the saintly gods that were guiding China once upon a time.

SAKAI

Yes. Thank you very much for coming today.

13

Creating a Society Where a Diversity Of Nations and Races Can Coexist

RYUHO OKAWA

[*Claps twice.*] It seemed as though he couldn't recall his memory of the past life as Sanai Hashimoto. He only passed, so this cannot be helped. He received international attention by winning a Nobel Peace Prize which is a big deal. So, by publishing this book of his, or if people listen to this spiritual message and so on in China, we might be able to build some sort of a "core." We must not cease to make efforts on this.

But we are not saying that we wish to annihilate China. We think that we must create a society where different nations and races can coexist. At a time when ballistic and nuclear missiles are being fortified, I do think that we need to have a deterrent ready. But I'm not saying this to annihilate those who oppose our way of thinking. I would be glad if we could notify the people of China that Happy Science isn't trying to Westernize nor is it a tyrannical nation of the East. It is teaching a new way of thinking. That is all. Thank you.

INTERVIEWERS

Thank you.

Afterword

Chinese tourists are coming to Japan and going on a shopping spree in Ginza, Shibuya, and Shinjuku. But if, on seeing them, we believe that China has finally joined the liberalist camp, we will eventually be faced with a huge problem. Last year, I went to New York and went up the Empire State Building. At that time, too, my group was the only Japanese one and others were mostly Chinese tourists. We can assume that some sort of national policy is behind this trend.

Liu Xiaobo, who just passed away the other day, was the flag-bearer of pro-democracy movement in China. The Chinese government dared to scatter his ashes, wiping out even the proof of his very existence. This nation does not understand that the goal of revolution is to achieve freedom; it still regards religion as opium and believes that national totalitarianism will make its people happy.

In a way, we can say that a devil is oppressing one-fifth of the human race. The Bible states that whoever does not love does not know God. To the believers of God all around the world, if you have a loving heart toward the people of China, please spread this gospel of resurrection of Liu Xiaobo, by all means. That is the very act of salvation.

Ryuho Okawa
Founder and CEO of Happy Science Group
July 23, 2017

ABOUT THE AUTHOR

Founder and CEO of Happy Science Group.

Ryuho Okawa was born on July 7th 1956, in Tokushima, Japan. After graduating from the University of Tokyo with a law degree, he joined a Tokyo-based trading house. While working at its New York headquarters, he studied international finance at the Graduate Center of the City University of New York. In 1981, he attained Great Enlightenment and became aware that he is El Cantare with a mission to bring salvation to all humankind.

In 1986, he established Happy Science. It now has members in over 165 countries across the world, with more than 700 branches and temples as well as 10,000 missionary houses around the world.

He has given over 3,450 lectures (of which more than 150 are in English) and published over 3,000 books (of which more than 600 are Spiritual Interview Series), and many are translated into 40 languages. Along with *The Laws of the Sun* and *The Laws Of Messiah*, many of the books have become best sellers or million sellers. To date, Happy Science has produced 25 movies. The original story and original concept were given by the Executive Producer Ryuho Okawa. He has also composed music and written lyrics of over 450 pieces.

Moreover, he is the Founder of Happy Science University and Happy Science Academy (Junior and Senior High School), Founder and President of the Happiness Realization Party, Founder and Honorary Headmaster of Happy Science Institute of Government and Management, Founder of IRH Press Co., Ltd., and the Chairperson of NEW STAR PRODUCTION Co., Ltd. and ARI Production Co., Ltd.

WHAT IS EL CANTARE?

El Cantare means "the Light of the Earth," and is the Supreme God of the Earth who has been guiding humankind since the beginning of Genesis. He is whom Jesus called Father and Muhammad called Allah, and is *Ame-no-Mioya-Gami*, Japanese Father God. Different parts of El Cantare's core consciousness have descended to Earth in the past, once as Alpha and another as Elohim. His branch spirits, such as Shakyamuni Buddha and Hermes, have descended to Earth many times and helped to flourish many civilizations. To unite various religions and to integrate various fields of study in order to build a new civilization on Earth, a part of the core consciousness has descended to Earth as Master Ryuho Okawa.

Alpha is a part of the core consciousness of El Cantare who descended to Earth around 330 million years ago. Alpha preached Earth's Truths to harmonize and unify Earth-born humans and space people who came from other planets.

Elohim is a part of El Cantare's core consciousness who descended to Earth around 150 million years ago. He gave wisdom, mainly on the differences of light and darkness, good and evil.

Ame-no-Mioya-Gami (Japanese Father God) is the Creator God and the Father God who appears in the ancient literature, *Hotsuma Tsutae*. It is believed that He descended on the foothills of Mt. Fuji about 30,000 years ago and built the Fuji dynasty, which is the root of the Japanese civilization. With justice as the central pillar, Ame-no-Mioya-Gami's teachings spread to ancient civilizations of other countries in the world.

Shakyamuni Buddha was born as a prince into the Shakya Clan in India around 2,600 years ago. When he was 29 years old, he renounced the world and sought enlightenment. He later attained Great Enlightenment and founded Buddhism.

Hermes is one of the 12 Olympian gods in Greek mythology, but the spiritual Truth is that he taught the teachings of love and progress around 4,300 years ago that became the origin of the current Western civilization. He is a hero that truly existed.

Ophealis was born in Greece around 6,500 years ago and was the leader who took an expedition to as far as Egypt. He is the God of miracles, prosperity, and arts, and is known as Osiris in the Egyptian mythology.

Rient Arl Croud was born as a king of the ancient Incan Empire around 7,000 years ago and taught about the mysteries of the mind. In the heavenly world, he is responsible for the interactions that take place between various planets.

Thoth was an almighty leader who built the golden age of the Atlantic civilization around 12,000 years ago. In the Egyptian mythology, he is known as god Thoth.

Ra Mu was a leader who built the golden age of the civilization of Mu around 17,000 years ago. As a religious leader and a politician, he ruled by uniting religion and politics.

WHAT IS A SPIRITUAL MESSAGE?

We are all spiritual beings living on this earth. The following is the mechanism behind Master Ryuho Okawa's spiritual messages.

1 You are a spirit

People are born into this world to gain wisdom through various experiences and return to the other world when their lives end. We are all spirits and repeat this cycle in order to refine our souls.

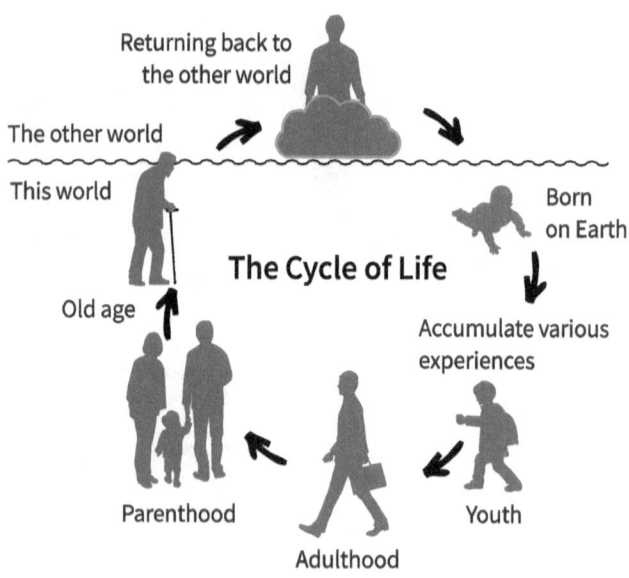

2 You have a guardian spirit

Guardian spirits are those who protect the people who are living on this earth. Each of us has a guardian spirit that watches over us and guides us from the other world. They were us in our past life, and are identical in how we think.

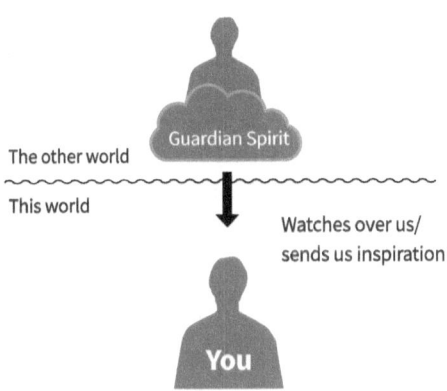

Guardian Spirit

The other world

This world

Watches over us/
sends us inspiration

You

3 How spiritual messages work

Master Ryuho Okawa, through his enlightenment, is capable of summoning any spirit from anywhere in the world, including the spirit world.

Master Okawa's way of receiving spiritual messages is fundamentally different from that of other psychic mediums who undergo trances and are thereby completely taken over by the spirits they are channeling.

Master Okawa's attainment of a high level of enlightenment enables him to retain full control of his consciousness and body throughout the duration of the spiritual message. To allow the spirits to express their own thoughts and personalities freely, however, Master Okawa usually softens the dominancy of his consciousness. This way, he is able to keep his own philosophies out of the way and ensure that the spiritual messages are pure expressions of the spirits he is channeling.

Since guardian spirits think at the same subconscious level as the person living on earth, Master Okawa can summon the spirit and find out what the person on earth is actually thinking. If the person has already returned to the other world, the spirit can give messages to the people living on earth through Master Okawa.

Since 2009, many spiritual messages have been openly recorded by Master Okawa and published. Spiritual messages from the guardian spirits of people living today such as Donald Trump, former Japanese Prime Minister Shinzo Abe and Chinese President Xi Jinping, as well as spiritual messages sent from the spirit world by Jesus Christ, Muhammad, Thomas Edison, Mother Teresa, Steve Jobs and Nelson Mandela are just a tiny pack of spiritual messages that were published so far.

Domestically, in Japan, these spiritual messages are being read by a wide range of politicians and mass media, and the high-level contents of these books are delivering an impact even more on politics, news and public opinion. In recent years, there have been spiritual messages recorded in English, and

English translations are being done on the spiritual messages given in Japanese. These have been published overseas, one after another, and have started to shake the world.

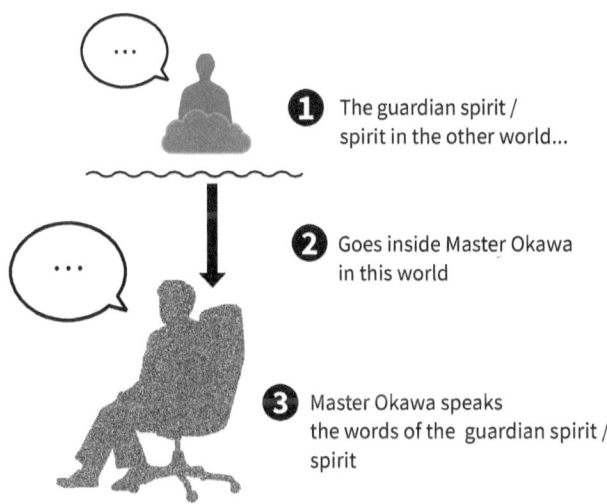

① The guardian spirit /
spirit in the other world...

② Goes inside Master Okawa
in this world

③ Master Okawa speaks
the words of the guardian spirit /
spirit

For more about spiritual messages and a complete list of books in the Spiritual Interview Series, visit okawabooks.com

ABOUT HAPPY SCIENCE

Happy Science is a global movement that empowers individuals to find purpose and spiritual happiness and to share that happiness with their families, societies, and the world. With more than 12 million members around the world, Happy Science aims to increase awareness of spiritual truths and expand our capacity for love, compassion, and joy so that together we can create the kind of world we all wish to live in.

Activities at Happy Science are based on the Principle of Happiness (Love, Wisdom, Self-Reflection, and Progress). This principle embraces worldwide philosophies and beliefs, transcending boundaries of culture and religions.

Love teaches us to give ourselves freely without expecting anything in return; it encompasses giving, nurturing, and forgiving.

Wisdom leads us to the insights of spiritual truths, and opens us to the true meaning of life and the will of God (the universe, the highest power, Buddha).

Self-Reflection brings a mindful, nonjudgmental lens to our thoughts and actions to help us find our truest selves—the essence of our souls—and deepen our connection to the highest power. It helps us attain a clean and peaceful mind and leads us to the right life path.

Progress emphasizes the positive, dynamic aspects of our spiritual growth—actions we can take to manifest and spread happiness around the world. It's a path that not only expands our soul growth, but also furthers the collective potential of the world we live in.

PROGRAMS AND EVENTS

The doors of Happy Science are open to all. We offer a variety of programs and events, including self-exploration and self-growth programs, spiritual seminars, meditation and contemplation sessions, study groups, and book events.

Our programs are designed to:
* Deepen your understanding of your purpose and meaning in life
* Improve your relationships and increase your capacity to love unconditionally
* Attain peace of mind, decrease anxiety and stress, and feel positive
* Gain deeper insights and a broader perspective on the world
* Learn how to overcome life's challenges
  ... and much more.

For more information, visit happy-science.org.

OUR ACTIVITIES

Happy Science does other various activities to provide support for those in need.

◆ **You Are An Angel! General Incorporated Association**

Happy Science has a volunteer network in Japan that encourages and supports children with disabilities as well as their parents and guardians.

◆ **Never Mind School for Truancy**

At 'Never Mind,' we support students who find it very challenging to attend schools in Japan. We also nurture their self-help spirit and power to rebound against obstacles in life based on Master Okawa's teachings and faith.

◆ **"Prevention Against Suicide" Campaign since 2003**

A nationwide campaign to reduce suicides; over 20,000 people commit suicide every year in Japan. "The Suicide Prevention Website-Words of Truth for You-" presents spiritual prescriptions for worries such as depression, lost love, extramarital affairs, bullying and work-related problems, thereby saving many lives.

◆ **Support for Anti-bullying Campaigns**

Happy Science provides support for a group of parents and guardians, Network to Protect Children from Bullying, a general incorporated foundation launched in Japan to end bullying, including those that can even be called a criminal offense. So far, the network received more than 5,000 cases and resolved 90% of them.

- **The Golden Age Scholarship**

  This scholarship is granted to students who can contribute greatly and bring a hopeful future to the world.

- **Success No.1**
  Buddha's Truth Afterschool Academy

  Happy Science has over 180 classrooms throughout Japan and in several cities around the world that focus on afterschool education for children. The education focuses on faith and morals in addition to supporting children's school studies.

- **Angel Plan V**

  For children under the age of kindergarten, Happy Science holds classes for nurturing healthy, positive, and creative boys and girls.

- **Future Stars Training Department**

  The Future Stars Training Department was founded within the Happy Science Media Division with the goal of nurturing talented individuals to become successful in the performing arts and entertainment industry.

- **NEW STAR PRODUCTION Co., Ltd.**
  ARI Production Co., Ltd.

  We have companies to nurture actors and actresses, artists, and vocalists. They are also involved in film production.

CONTACT INFORMATION

Happy Science is a worldwide organization with branches and temples around the globe. For a comprehensive list, visit the worldwide directory at *happy-science.org*. The following are some of the many Happy Science locations:

UNITED STATES AND CANADA

New York
79 Franklin St., New York, NY 10013, USA
Phone: 1-212-343-7972
Fax: 1-212-343-7973
Email: ny@happy-science.org
Website: happyscience-usa.org

New Jersey
66 Hudson St., #2R, Hoboken, NJ 07030, USA
Phone: 1-201-313-0127
Email: nj@happy-science.org
Website: happyscience-usa.org

Chicago
2300 Barrington Rd., Suite #400,
Hoffman Estates, IL 60169, USA
Phone: 1-630-937-3077
Email: chicago@happy-science.org
Website: happyscience-usa.org

Florida
5208 8th St., Zephyrhills, FL 33542, USA
Phone: 1-813-715-0000
Fax: 1-813-715-0010
Email: florida@happy-science.org
Website: happyscience-usa.org

Atlanta
1874 Piedmont Ave., NE Suite 360-C
Atlanta, GA 30324, USA
Phone: 1-404-892-7770
Email: atlanta@happy-science.org
Website: happyscience-usa.org

San Francisco
525 Clinton St.
Redwood City, CA 94062, USA
Phone & Fax: 1-650-363-2777
Email: sf@happy-science.org
Website: happyscience-usa.org

Los Angeles
1590 E. Del Mar Blvd., Pasadena, CA 91106, USA
Phone: 1-626-395-7775
Fax: 1-626-395-7776
Email: la@happy-science.org
Website: happyscience-usa.org

Orange County
16541 Gothard St. Suite 104
Huntington Beach, CA 92647
Phone: 1-714-659-1501
Email: oc@happy-science.org
Website: happyscience-usa.org

San Diego
7841 Balboa Ave. Suite #202
San Diego, CA 92111, USA
Phone: 1-626-395-7775
Fax: 1-626-395-7776
E-mail: sandiego@happy-science.org
Website: happyscience-usa.org

Hawaii
Phone: 1-808-591-9772
Fax: 1-808-591-9776
Email: hi@happy-science.org
Website: happyscience-usa.org

Kauai
3343 Kanakolu Street, Suite 5
Lihue, HI 96766, USA
Phone: 1-808-822-7007
Fax: 1-808-822-6007
Email: kauai-hi@happy-science.org
Website: happyscience-usa.org

Toronto

845 The Queensway
Etobicoke, ON M8Z 1N6, Canada
Phone: 1-416-901-3747
Email: toronto@happy-science.org
Website: happy-science.ca

Vancouver

#201-2607 East 49th Avenue,
Vancouver, BC, V5S 1J9, Canada
Phone: 1-604-437-7735
Fax: 1-604-437-7764
Email: vancouver@happy-science.org
Website: happy-science.ca

INTERNATIONAL

Tokyo

1-6-7 Togoshi, Shinagawa,
Tokyo, 142-0041, Japan
Phone: 81-3-6384-5770
Fax: 81-3-6384-5776
Email: tokyo@happy-science.org
Website: happy-science.org

Seoul

74, Sadang-ro 27-gil,
Dongjak-gu, Seoul, Korea
Phone: 82-2-3478-8777
Fax: 82-2-3478-9777
Email: korea@happy-science.org
Website: happyscience-korea.org

London

3 Margaret St.
London, W1W 8RE United Kingdom
Phone: 44-20-7323-9255
Fax: 44-20-7323-9344
Email: eu@happy-science.org
Website: www.happyscience-uk.org

Taipei

No. 89, Lane 155, Dunhua N. Road,
Songshan District, Taipei City 105, Taiwan
Phone: 886-2-2719-9377
Fax: 886-2-2719-5570
Email: taiwan@happy-science.org
Website: happyscience-tw.org

Sydney

516 Pacific Highway, Lane Cove North,
2066 NSW, Australia
Phone: 61-2-9411-2877
Fax: 61-2-9411-2822
Email: sydney@happy-science.org

Kuala Lumpur

No 22A, Block 2, Jalil Link Jalan Jalil
Jaya 2, Bukit Jalil 57000,
Kuala Lumpur, Malaysia
Phone: 60-3-8998-7877
Fax: 60-3-8998-7977
Email: malaysia@happy-science.org
Website: happyscience.org.my

Sao Paulo

Rua. Domingos de Morais 1154,
Vila Mariana, Sao Paulo SP
CEP 04010-100, Brazil
Phone: 55-11-5088-3800
Email: sp@happy-science.org
Website: happyscience.com.br

Kathmandu

Kathmandu Metropolitan City,
Ward No. 15, Ring Road, Kimdol,
Sitapaila Kathmandu, Nepal
Phone: 977-1-427-2931
Email: nepal@happy-science.org

Jundiai

Rua Congo, 447, Jd. Bonfiglioli
Jundiai-CEP, 13207-340, Brazil
Phone: 55-11-4587-5952
Email: jundiai@happy-science.org

Kampala

Plot 877 Rubaga Road, Kampala
P.O. Box 34130 Kampala, UGANDA
Phone: 256-79-4682-121
Email: uganda@happy-science.org

ABOUT HAPPINESS REALIZATION PARTY

The Happiness Realization Party (HRP) was founded in May 2009 by Master Ryuho Okawa as part of the Happy Science Group. HRP strives to improve the Japanese society, based on three basic political principles of "freedom, democracy, and faith," and let Japan promote individual and public happiness from Asia to the world as a leader nation.

1) Diplomacy and Security: Protecting Freedom, Democracy, and Faith of Japan and the World from China's Totalitarianism

Japan's current defense system is insufficient against China's expanding hegemony and the threat of North Korea's nuclear missiles. Japan, as the leader of Asia, must strengthen its defense power and promote strategic diplomacy together with the nations which share the values of freedom, democracy, and faith. Further, HRP aims to realize world peace under the leadership of Japan, the nation with the spirit of religious tolerance.

2) Economy: Early economic recovery through utilizing the "wisdom of the private sector"

Economy has been damaged severely by the novel coronavirus originated in China. Many companies have been forced into bankruptcy or out of business. What is needed for economic recovery now is not subsidies and regulations by the government, but policies which can utilize the "wisdom of the private sector."

For more information, visit en.hr-party.jp

HAPPY SCIENCE ACADEMY JUNIOR AND SENIOR HIGH SCHOOL

Happy Science Academy Junior and Senior High School is a boarding school founded with the goal of educating the future leaders of the world who can have a big vision, persevere, and take on new challenges.

Currently, there are two campuses in Japan; the Nasu Main Campus in Tochigi Prefecture, founded in 2010, and the Kansai Campus in Shiga Prefecture, founded in 2013.

Nasu Main Campus

Kansai Campus

 HAPPY SCIENCE UNIVERSITY

THE FOUNDING SPIRIT AND THE GOAL OF EDUCATION

Based on the founding philosophy of the university, "Exploration of happiness and the creation of a new civilization," education, research and studies will be provided to help students acquire deep understanding grounded in religious belief and advanced expertise with the objectives of producing "great talents of virtue" who can contribute in a broad-ranging way to serve Japan and the international society.

FACULTIES

Faculty of human happiness

Students in this faculty will pursue liberal arts from various perspectives with a multidisciplinary approach, explore and envision an ideal state of human beings and society.

Faculty of successful management

This faculty aims to realize successful management that helps organizations to create value and wealth for society and to contribute to the happiness and the development of management and employees as well as society as a whole.

Faculty of future creation

Students in this faculty study subjects such as political science, journalism, performing arts and artistic expression, and explore and present new political and cultural models based on truth, goodness and beauty.

Faculty of future industry

This faculty aims to nurture engineers who can resolve various issues facing modern civilization from a technological standpoint and contribute to the creation of new industries of the future.

ABOUT HS PRESS

HS Press is an imprint of IRH Press Co., Ltd. IRH Press Co., Ltd., based in Tokyo, was founded in 1987 as a publishing division of Happy Science. IRH Press publishes religious and spiritual books, journals, magazines and also operates broadcast and film production enterprises. For more information, visit *okawabooks.com*.

Follow us on:

f Facebook: Okawa Books   **○** Instagram: OkawaBooks

▶ Youtube: Okawa Books   **y** Twitter: Okawa Books

𝓟 Pinterest: Okawa Books   **g** Goodreads: Ryuho Okawa

——— **NEWSLETTER** ———

To receive book related news, promotions and events, please subscribe to our newsletter below.

∞ eepurl.com/bsMeJj

 ——— **AUDIO / VISUAL MEDIA** ———

YOUTUBE   **PODCAST**

Introduction of Ryuho Okawa's titles; topics ranging from self-help, current affairs, spirituality, religion, and the universe.

BOOKS BY RYUHO OKAWA

THE LAWS OF MISSION

ESSENTIAL TRUTHS FOR SPIRITUAL AWAKENING IN A SECULAR AGE

In this day and age of advanced scientific and information technology, we are often deluded by a false sense that we know everything. But in fact, many people cannot even answer simple but fundamental questions about life, such as "what's the purpose of our life" and "what happens after death."

In this book, Ryuho Okawa offers integral spiritual truths that bring about spiritual awakening within each of us. This book helps us find the purpose and meaning of our life and make the right decisions so that we can walk on the path to happiness.

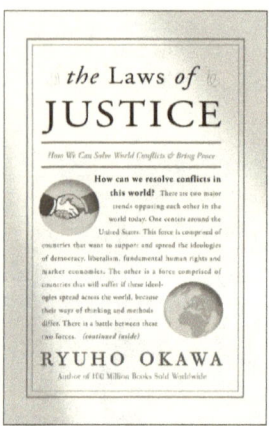

THE LAWS OF JUSTICE
HOW WE CAN SOLVE
WORLD CONFLICTS & BRING PEACE

How can we solve conflicts in this world? Why is it that we continue to live in a world of turmoil, when we all wish to live in a world of peace and harmony?

In recent years, we've faced issues that jeopardize international peace and security, including the rise of ISIS, Syrian civil war and refugee crisis, break-off of diplomatic relations between Saudi Arabia and Iran, Russia's annexation of Crimea, China's military expansion, and North Korea's nuclear development.

This book shows what global justice is from a comprehensive perspective of the Supreme God. Becoming aware of this view will let us embrace differences in beliefs, recognize other people's divine nature, and love and forgive one another. It will also become the key to solving the issues we face, whether they're religious, political, societal, economic, or academic, and help the world become a better and safer world for all of us living today.

THE TRUMP SECRET

SEEING THROUGH THE PAST, PRESENT, AND FUTURE
OF THE NEW AMERICAN PRESIDENT

Donald Trump's victory in the 2016 presidential election surprised almost all major vote forecasters who predicted Hillary Clinton's victory. But 10 months earlier, in January 2016, Ryuho Okawa, Global Visionary, a renowned spiritual leader, and international best-selling author, had already foreseen Trump's victory. This book contains a series of lectures and interviews that unveil the secrets to Trump's victory and makes predictions of what will happen under his presidency. This book predicts the coming of a new America that will go through a great transformation from the "red and blue states" to the United States.

CONTENTS

THE LAWS OF THE SUN

ONE SOURCE, ONE PLANET, ONE PEOPLE

IMAGINE IF YOU COULD ASK GOD why He created this world and what spiritual laws He used to shape us—and everything around us. If we could understand His designs and intentions, we could discover what our goals in life should be and whether our actions move us closer to those goals or farther away.

THE GOLDEN LAWS

HISTORY THROUGH THE EYES OF THE ETERNAL BUDDHA

The Golden Laws reveals how Buddha's Plan has been unfolding on earth, and outlines five thousand years of the secret history of humankind. Once we understand the true course of history, we cannot help but become aware of the significance of our spiritual mission in the present age.

THE NINE DIMENSIONS

UNVEILING THE LAWS OF ETERNITY

This book is a window into the mind of our loving God, who encourages us to grow into greater angels. It reveals His deepest intentions, answering the timely question of why He conceived such a colorful medley of religions, philosophies, sciences, arts, and other forms of expression.

For a complete list of books, visit okawabooks.com

THE MANIFESTO OF THE HAPPINESS REALIZATION PARTY

This book is a historical declaration to change the world through a peaceful revolution by the philosophy and speech based on the Truth, rather than by violence or massacre. It also states on the assessment of the meaning of WWII as well as how the relation between religion and politics should be. It is a must read for all people who wish to build a true utopia.

THE DECISION TOWARD PROSPERITY

THE TRUMP REVOLUTION WILL CHANGE THE WORLD

In the book, Okawa talks a lot about Japanese politics as Japan is his mother country, but the universal philosophy behind his words will surely enlighten readers in other countries too. This is the guidebook that will help the world realize prosperity for the next 300 years.

INTO THE STORM OF INTERNATIONAL POLITICS

THE NEW STANDARDS OF THE WORLD ORDER

The world is now seeking a new idea or a new philosophy. In this book, Okawa presents new standards of the world order while giving his own analysis on world affairs concerning the U.S., China, Islamic State and others.

For a complete list of books, visit okawabooks.com

CRITIQUE OF CURRENT WORLD AFFAIRS

IMMANUEL KANT'S ADVICE FROM HEAVEN

"We can clearly see from Kant's message that we constantly need to enlighten people in order to prevent humankind from falling into a dangerous, hellish way of thinking."

—From Preface

[This book is available only in local branches and temples. Please refer to the contact information.]

ON HAPPINESS REVOLUTION

A SPIRITUAL INTERVIEW WITH HANNAH ARENDT

In this book, the German-born Jewish American political theorist offers a spiritual lecture on democracy, on totalitarianism in East Asia, on communism and equality, on the Love of God and Justice of God, as well as her mission as a prophet of the new age.

NELSON MANDELA'S LAST MESSAGE
A CONVERSATION WITH MADIBA
SIX HOURS AFTER HIS DEATH

As Mandela's spirit says in this spiritual interview, God created our souls as thinking energy without color, and that our colorless soul is the basis of our fundamental freedom and equality. In this spiritual interview, Master Ryuho Okawa gives us a glimpse into the mind of this great leader whose undefeated spirit is a message of hope to us all.

For a complete list of books, visit okawabooks.com

CHINA'S HIDDEN AGENDA

THE MASTERMIND BEHIND THE ANTI-AMERICAN AND ANTI-JAPANESE PROTESTS

"I wanted to stir up the anti-American movement in the Arab world to make sure that the United States won't be able to attack Syria or Iran...I'm the mastermind behind the Muhammad video."

—Xi Jinping's Guardian Spirit

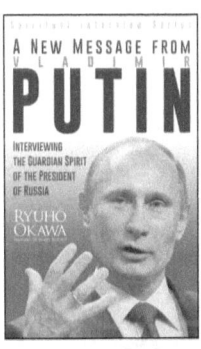

A NEW MESSAGE FROM VLADIMIR PUTIN

INVERVIEWING THE GUARDIAN SPIRIT OF THE PRESIDENT OF RUSSIA

We hereby bring you the spiritual message from the guardian spirit of President Putin, the politician who is the center of attention of not just the people of Russia but of the whole world, regardless of it being in a good or a bad way. In the Preface, it says, "President Putin's true intentions, which are 90 percent misunderstood."

EXPOSING NORTH KOREA'S MENACING LEADER

KIM JONG UN'S PLOT FOR A PSYCHOLOGICAL WAR

This book reveals the role that North Korea is playing in China's imperialistic strategy and the two nations' close ties with Iran. Together, China and Kim Jong Un are carrying out a psychological war that takes full advantage of the weaknesses of Japanese Prime Minister Abe and United States President Obama.

For a complete list of books, visit okawabooks.com

127